Front Cover:
*The Langdale Pikes and
Herdwicks — Kendal Auction Mart*

Back cover:
A Last Word

FACES OF LAKELAND

Photographs by John & Eliza Forder
Text by Arthur Raistrick

We would like to dedicate this book to all those who live in Lakeland, and offer them our warmest thanks for the help they have given us while photographing, with particular gratitude to Richard and Barbara Charnley.

We would also like to thank Northern Arts, Ilford Ltd., The National Trust, and Richard David for their invaluable support, without which this book would not have been possible.

ISBN 0 948511 25 7

Published by
Frank Peters Publishing Ltd.
Kendal, Cumbria

Printed by
Frank Peters Printers Ltd.
Kendal, Cumbria

Designed by
Ram Design Associates Ltd.
Kendal, Cumbria

THE PHOTOGRAPHS

CONTENTS

The photographs are divided into Two
Sections: 'The Land' and
            'The Life'

BIOGRAPHIES

Arthur Raistrick was born in Saltaire in 1896. After Bradford Grammar School he was apprenticed as an engineer and later graduated from the University of Leeds with an M.Sc. in engineering and a Ph.D. in geology. He spent a few years in research in coal technology before becoming lecturer and later Reader in Applied Geology in Mining and Engineering at King's College, now the University of Newcastle.

His working life and all his leisure have been devoted to research on many aspects of the history and geography of northern England, for forty-five years in partnership with his wife Elizabeth, a graduate in geology. These studies have inspired a great number of books — *The Pennine Dales, Industrial Archaeology, Old Yorkshire Dales, The Nature and Origin of Coal* — and other publications, whose worth has been recognized by many awards from learned societies and by honorary degrees from Leeds and Bradford Universities.

A Dalesman and a Quaker, Arthur Raistrick is widely known and revered, not only for his learning and his ability to communicate it agreeably, but also for qualities characteristic of those callings: integrity, unswerving convictions, generosity and an intense local pride.

John and Eliza Forder have lived for over twelve years in Dentdale, one of the remoter dales on the eastern border of Cumbria, where they have a small studio. Self-taught photographers, they feel the black and white medium is particularly appropriate to convey the moods and shapes of the northern hill country and the character of its people. Their first book, *Open Fell Hidden Dale*, a portrayal of the life and landscape of the Yorkshire Dales, (also with text by Arthur Raistrick), was published in 1985 and exhibitions of its photographs have been mounted in London, Bradford, Harrogate, Kendal and many other places in the north. The photographs for *Faces of Lakeland* have all been taken within the last two years.

INTRODUCTION

For more than two centuries Lakeland, or the Lake District, has been a name commonly applied to the central mass of Cumbrian mountains, but surrounding this lie parts of old Cumberland, Westmorland and Lancashire that are historically and culturally linked to the better known land of mountains and lakes. The boundaries of this larger Lake District stretch as far east as the Cross Fell scarp of the Pennines, on the west to the Cumbrian coast, on the north to the Solway Firth, and on the south as far as Morecambe Bay. Although these areas differ in appearance, and also breed varying lifestyles, they are all interdependent.

During several thousand years this environment has been a homeland in which people of differing origins, from prehistoric to Celtic, Anglian and Norse, have found their living, and from the mingling of these many sources has come a 'native' Cumbrian stock. An original cover of forest has gradually been cleared to free arable and pasture land. Farms, hamlets and villages have been settled. The raw materials — timber, stone from the fells and minerals — have been exploited to enrich the conditions of life not only in Lakeland but outside it, and in the last two centuries an increasing number of visitors has found both recreation and inspiration among the dramatic beauty of the fells, and they too have contributed to the economy of the area.

The rugged crags, the gentler valleys and lakes, the tumbling waterfalls, and changeable mountain weather present each one of us with lingering memories of Lakeland's many facets. The visitors carry these experiences home with them, while those who live and work there are absorbed by them and express them in their daily lives with qualities such as endurance, independence and good humour as well as an increasing aptitude to share their heritage with visitors.

For each one of us Lakeland offers something different, and in the following pages these varying aspects have been knit together. In the text are described the complexities of the geology and history of the central and outlying areas, while attention is also drawn to the issues facing Lakelanders in the late twentieth century. The photographs not only portray the landscape of the central hill area through the seasons and in varying weathers, but also allow a glimpse of the life that goes on there, behind the veils of the mountain mists.

MAP OF LAKELAND

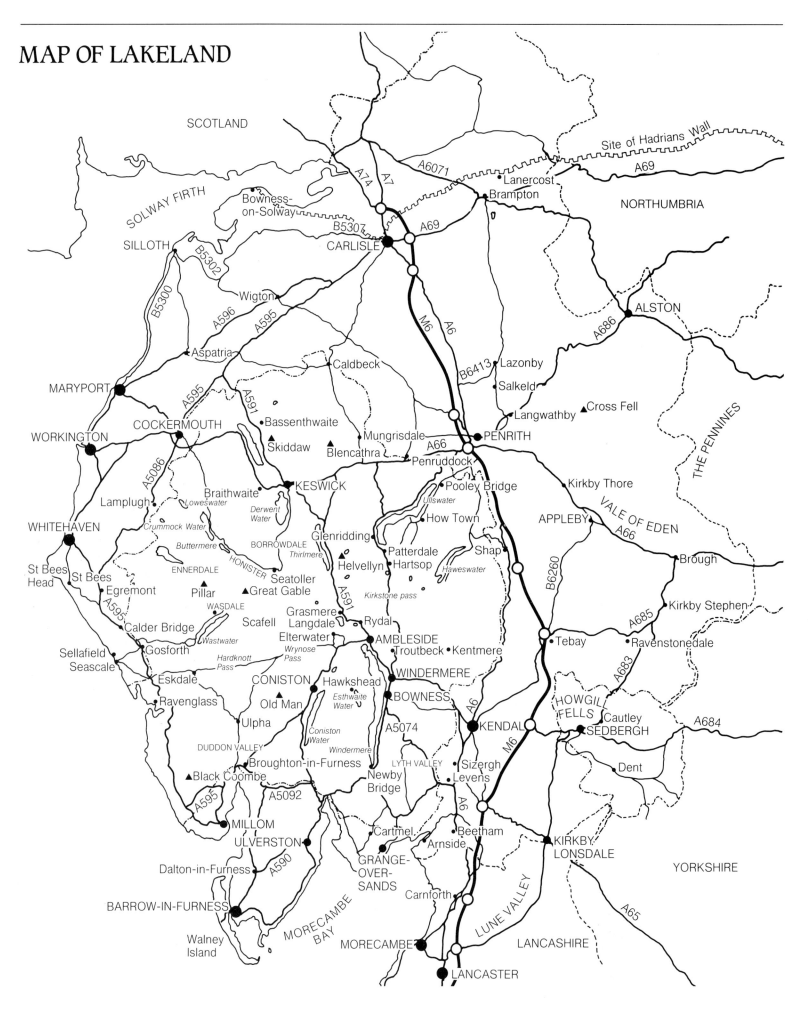

THE STORY OF LAKELAND
The Foundations

The geology of the Lake District, the underlying and dominating foundation of all the physical features, is very complex and is still the subject of extensive research, involving many new techniques and ideas that have been developed during the last few decades and can be justly described as revolutionary. It will serve our purpose to give only a bare outline of the story that is emerging and of the almost unimaginable events the evidence for which and their consequences is only now being recognised and interpreted. If we confine the story to that part of the Earth's history represented by the visible rocks of the Lake District it will still take us back in time for some five hundred million years. The Lake District rocks were principally formed in the period between five hundred and two hundred million years ago. After this formative period there is a gap from which no rocks remain, and only the last two million years have left a thin covering mask of more recent deposits. These are the clays, gravels and sands left by the Ice Age, but at that time there also occurred considerable erosion with much moulding of the landscape and the formation of the lakes, tarns and sharp edges that today are principal features in the scenery.

The oldest rocks in the Lake District are those of the period named, by our almost local Adam Sedgwick of Dent, the Ordovician. Sedgwick made a detailed study of the Lake District rocks, elucidating their structure and outlining their history, and he gave the first description of them to the Geological Society of London in 1835 and again to his friend Wordsworth in letters that were printed in Wordsworth's *Guide to the Lake District* (1859). The Ordovician rocks, which make up the bulk of Skiddaw and Blencathra and the northern part of the area, also form Black Combe in the south-west. Within the last fifty years geologists, with their new methods and concepts, have identified the ocean in which these rocks were formed and have given it the name Iapetus. Into this ocean came rock detritus carried by rivers from two continents, east and west, Iapetus being an ocean very much on the line of the present Atlantic. An earlier continental mass covering both Eurasia and America had been split by earth movements along a line north-east to south-west. This line was in part roughly on the Solway Firth, leaving a slice of Norway, most of Scotland and part of Northern Ireland to the western land-mass, with the Lake District as part of its eastern continental shelf, while the rest of England and Wales remained part of the Eurasian continent. Continued earth movements began the closure of Iapetus but this was not accomplished until the end of the Silurian time, about four hundred million years ago.

The two drifting continental masses in their approach and eventual collision created belts of gigantic volcanoes down the continental edges, one of which passed through the Lake District and so piled up the next set of rocks. The Borrowdale Volcanic group comprises nearly sixteen thousand feet of volcanic lavas, with interbedded layers of 'ash', out of which is carved the central mountain mass, Gable, Scafell, Helvellyn and all the other great peaks. Some of the volcanoes were submarine, some were on shore, and they were not alone for there were other volcanoes in Wales and Ireland belonging to the same group. The mind boggles as we try to picture these vast earth-shaking and shaping events, which occupied about fifty million years. As one stands on a mountain of volcanic lavas, say Gable, one must be deeply stirred by the wonder that is the proper due of the scenery.

The violence of the Ordovician period was followed by a quiet age, the Silurian, which lasted fifty million years. During this time several thousand feet of detritus were deposited in the last phase of Iapetus, producing the sedimentary rocks, limestone, sandstone and shales, that make up the southern part of the Lake District. The first deposit is the thin layer of Coniston Limestone, which extends from the head of the Duddon estuary, past the head of Coniston Water, and then by the head of Windermere to Shap on the western edge of the Vale of Eden. The more sandy deposits, now about ten thousand feet of sandstone and grits, lie on the south side of this, embracing the whole of Coniston Water, Elterwater and Windermere. To the south again the sandstones are covered by the Carboniferous Limestones of the northern side of Morecambe Bay. This part of the Silurian makes the rich well-wooded country from the Duddon estuary to the Howgill Fells and from Ulverston by Kendal to Sedbergh.

The final collision of the two continents was no sudden catastrophe but rather a very slow battle of gigantic forces over several scores of millions of years. The thrusting of the masses against each other resulted in what is called the Caledonian Orogeny, or mountain folding. The name was given because the folding raised great mountain chains originally at least on the scale of the present Himalayas, and because, although they extended north-east to south-west from Norway to Wales, they were first studied in Scotland. Their southern edge included the folds of the Lake District. During a few tens of millions of years these mountains were being eroded, carved and worn by weather and rivers until they were ground down to a low undulating hilly surface: a continental area that — in contrast with all the preceding times — was an arid, waterless desert. This period is called the Devonian. There were Devonian seas to the south, in which life was abundant and evolution continued on its way. It might be well to examine for a few minutes what living creatures were in existence through all these times.

The first signs of life, the first living cells to leave any record in the rocks, date back some three thousand million years; but before two thousand million years ago combinations of cells recognisable as plants had evolved along with the blue-green algae and bacteria. By the time of the oldest rocks we know in the Lake District, five hundred million years ago, evolution had progressed a long way and the seas were inhabited by animals with more than a simple cell structure whose fossils can be collected from Ordovician rocks. During all the events we have so far contemplated, evolution pursued its course and the muds of the Skiddaw Slates contain more complex animals, single and bivalve shellfish being abundant. Trilobites, even more complex and related to the crabs, lobsters and shrimps of today, crawled in the bottom muds, and a group of animals that became dominant in the Silurian, the graptolites, appeared before the end of the Ordovician. These were colonies of comparatively simple creatures, living in small horny pockets strung along and connected to a common canal, which had at one end a float. The strings, one or more together, hung down in the surface waters and their fossils are found in many of the softer shales. Other quite complicated animals such as primitive corals were evolving in the late Ordovician and became abundant in upper Silurian. Along with them were a small group of chordates, that is animals with a notochord, the prototype of the backbone, and from these, by the Devonian time, the first true vertebrates, the fishes, had evolved in several forms.

To return now to the story of the rocks and to the Caledonian Orogeny, the great event at the end of the Silurian period. The net effects of this were very complex. All the rocks of the Lake District were folded and faulted and many of them were metamorphosed — that is their nature was altered by the effects of great pressure and movement. Several of the beds of fine ash within the volcanic groups of the Borrowdale series were cleaved to form slates. The cleavages are not simple but many of them produced slates of fine quality. These gave the district one of its oldest industries, extending through almost all its history and still important today when the slates of Kirkstone, Honister, Walney and a few others are of nearly worldwide esteem. The granite of Shap is equally famous today, and for a few centuries copper and lead provided a flourishing industry.

In the latter part of the orogeny the intrusion of a vast body of granite under most of the Lake District raised it into a large dome. This mass of granite extended from near the present west coast eastward as far as Wear Dale and at its widest from Skiddaw south almost to Ambleside; but it was very much dumb-bell shaped, with the narrow part near Shap. High peaks on the granite mass are now exposed as the Eskdale, Skiddaw and Shap granites, and there are several other much smaller outcrops. Later, as the granite cooled, it was responsible for much of the mineralisation of the overlying strata.

At the final closing up of the ocean Iapetus a large continental mass, extending from western Canada to Russia, was formed and through most of the succeeding forty million years a large part of it constituted the Devonian desert in which there was an accumulation of red sands. None of these remained, however, after the heavy erosion that persisted throughout the area. The period that followed the Devonian was the

Carboniferous, so called because it produced the Coal Measures that make the coal fields. The dome of the Lake District for long remained above the growing seas of the Carboniferous and only slowly, with subsidence, was it finally submerged in a sea in which the upper part of the limestones could be deposited. There was much variation in levels, and two deep troughs were formed north and south of the Lake District to the Howgill Fells ridge. In these there was a thick deposit of Carboniferous strata. The lower Carboniferous sea was warm and clear, and this made possible extensive growth of corals and of diatoms and foraminifera, microscopic plants and animals that flourished in such enormous quantity that their remains made up the greater part of a calcareous mud, the parent of the limestones that surround the dome of older rocks. Evolution had proceeded further, and there were many types of fish in these seas and early forms of amphibia. On emergent land areas plants had spread to form primitive forests, which in the upper Carboniferous provided the material that made the coal seams of the Coal Measures that still lie along the north-western and western sides of the present Lake District.

With later changes of level the limestones of the lower Carboniferous emerged, and despite subsequent erosions survive as the fine landmarks of the southern area, such as Whitbarrow Scar. There is also a belt of limestone features lying along the western side of the Vale of Eden, and another narrow belt along the northern and north-western boundaries of the district. Besides creating scenic effect, the limestones or part of them are the site of the principal iron ore fields of the north-west and of part of Furness.

At the end of the Carboniferous period there was another age of earth movements when the great ocean of Tethys, which ran across the south of the Eurasian continent between it and Africa, was closing up. The so-called Hercynian folding caused by these movements was effective in elevating the Pennines but was only slightly felt in the Lake District, merely increasing its doming and causing the Carboniferous rocks to dip at low angles off the dome. The great mass of granite underlying all from Ennerdale to Wear Dale made the Lake District and the north Pennines a rigid block, and so minimised the effects of the folding. For the next seventy-five million years or so the area was again a fairly low continental mass, and the two periods of the Permian and Triassic were desert. They produced the red sandstones of the Vale of Eden and the northern plain and the St Bees sandstone of the mid-western coastal strip. Besides the fine building stone from these sandstones, to be seen in, among others, the lovely red buildings of Penrith and Brough castles, the upper part of the Permian in the Vale of Eden includes extensive beds of gypsum, which was quarried and mined around Kirkby Thore. The Permian is probably also the source of the iron ore deposits in both the north-western and southern areas.

A period of just short of two hundred million years followed the Trias, and it is likely that during a part of that time some later deposits, almost certainly the Chalk, covered the whole Lake District but was subsequently removed by erosion leaving the district very much as we now know it. During that long interval, however, two geological events occurred, which must be mentioned for their interest and importance. The American-Eurasian continent was again split by fresh movements of the crust, the sections drifted apart and the Atlantic Ocean was born and began to widen, a process that is still continuing. At the same time a northward drifting of the European mass ended the desert conditions and brought us into the zone of temperate climates.

After the Permio-Triassic came the Jurassic period, the 'Age of the Dinosaurs'; and then the Cretaceous during which the Lake District was probably again under a shallow ocean and receiving a thick covering of chalk. There are now no traces of any of these beds in our area, though the chalk makes the great cliffs around Flamborough. The penultimate geological epoch was the Tertiary, during part of which the present doming of the Lake District was completed and its rivers were initiated and began cutting their present pattern of nearly radial valleys.

The last two million years or so are known as the Quaternary Period, which includes the great Ice Age, and it is to this that we owe a large part of the beautiful detail of the scenery. The lakes occupy valleys superdeepened by the grinding of glacier ice: the floor of Windermere lies around a hundred feet below present sea level and Wastwater is much deeper. The tarns, which are on most of the mountains, are the corries scooped out by ice and where, as frequently, they impinge on one another they have produced the many 'edges', for example Striding Edge and Swirral Edge between the three corries of Nethermost Cove, Red Cove and Keppel Cove. The rounded smooth summits of many mountains, for example Great Gable and Blencathra, are the result of ice erosion; valleys have been smoothed and moulded to a U-shape with steepened sides down which streams tumble in the numerous waterfalls. It was the glaciers that deposited the many morainic mounds of gravel and sand in the upper part of valleys (Langdale has fine examples) and the wider thick sheets of boulder clay spread over most of the lowlands and contributing to the thick soils of the farming areas, so rich in the Vale of Eden and the northern plain.

As the last glaciers of the corries waned and disappeared and the climate improved, vegetation crept back, forests invaded the valleys and mountain sides and the heights grew thin scrub. All these provided hunting ground for the earliest human settlers of whom we have knowledge. These settlers made the district their home in the three or four millennia prior to the years A.D.

The Human Invasion

The ending of the Ice Age overlapped the beginning of human historic time. Climatic evidence in peat and in lake deposits suggests an ending of glacial time at about 8,000 B.C. The earliest human immigrants reached Lake District shores some long time after this, to be followed by the invasions of many different peoples during some three or four thousand years B.C., all making their contribution to the essential character of the 'native' Lakeland population. None of the 'invasions' was warlike, none was sudden, all were very much the natural spread of peoples under the pressure of an increasing population combined with a growing spirit of adventure. Adventurers generation after generation would push a little further than their fathers had done into the virgin land; old settlement was stabilised, new settlement started. Inevitably, once settlement had been made, the preconditions existed for dispute and conquest, but in the wild country of the Lake District any picture of invading and warring armies would be wrong.

Where archaeological excavation has provided remains of organic materials or charcoal, the modern techniques of radio carbon dating enable us to speak with increasingly close approximation to true dates. The earliest arrivals in the area were members of the Mesolithic folk, makers of minute flint implements, followers on from the Palaeolithic or Old Stone Age peoples. Some of them settled on Walney Island, some at Ehenside and some at Barfield Tarn. Materials from the Ehenside site give dates of about 3000 to 1600 B.C., so that we can take the arrival of these settlers as having been some time before 3000 B.C. and possibly even before 4000 B.C. The forests had returned to the country and would have been principally of birch, with some pine and hazel, oak and ash, extending up to about 2000 feet above sea level. There is growing evidence that the colonists made small clearings in the edge of the forest that encouraged the red deer to browse.

These Mesolithic folk were quickly followed by the people of the New Stone Age (Neolithic) in much larger numbers during the third millennium B.C. In many of their ways they were revolutionary: though still hunters and fishermen they were first and foremost farmers, growing grains, domesticating sheep and cattle, and breeding dogs. They also knew how to use fire to make pottery. Little need be said here about their way of life as there is an abundant modern literature on the subject. Some features of their settlement in the Lake District are, however, worthy of brief comment. Their settlements were made on the richer valley bottoms and on the good soils of the peripheral areas where tiny plots might be cultivated and where on the lower hill-slopes woodland could be cleared in patches, either by burning or by the use of their stone axes. They settled, probably as related or family groups, in single farms or in small clusters of huts built of timber and wattle on a stone foundation ring. A few larger settlements were proto-villages. The foundations of many of these are still to be seen, some with a surrounding bank, a defensive palisade against wolves and bears rather than against men. On several hill-tops there are larger structures, hill forts where a large number of folk and stock might take refuge in time of danger. The stone axes used in their attack on the woodlands were made locally and became their first article of industry and trade. Some who came into Langdale either as prospectors or as settlers discovered, in a high gully and its screes at over 1000 feet on the front of Pike of Stickle, large supplies of one of the metamorphosed volcanic ashes of very fine grain and great toughness. This they both collected and quarried and from it chipped rough stone axes. By modern dating, this work was going on between 2750 and 2550 B.C., but would have begun before the first date and continued later than the second. A few other similar locations were also found and worked. It is probable that the 'roughs' were got in summer and reserved in part for grinding and polishing during the inclement winter days. Many were traded over much of Britain even as far south as the Thames valley, and there is evidence that many were sharpened at their final destination. During this period the climate was getting warmer and small settlements, farms, with their enclosures for stock and cultivation, were being established on suitable ground.

The Neolithic people encountered another wave of immigrants, the Bronze Age folk, carriers of some of the Mediterranean technologies among which was a great skill in metallurgy and some tradition of building large stone megalithic structures. About 1800 B.C. they arrived with bronze swords and axes, a superiority that along with their greater degree of organisation enabled them quickly to become a ruling aristocracy among the neolithic folk, using them as serfs or slave-like servants. With these as labourers they built some of the finest of the prehistoric monuments that survive for our admiration and wonder, the large stone circles. Their purpose and use may still be the subject of speculation, argument and legend, but the interest that they arouse is a valuable part of our heritage.

These Bronze Age people came to the Lake District in three ways: by the Tyne Valley, by the Stainmore Pass and via the Irish Sea and the Isle of Man to the Lancashire and south Cumberland coast as far north as St Bees. They too settled in general in the lowland valleys and occupied two principal areas where their remains, burial mounds and small burial circles, are particularly numerous. These areas are the southern and western parts of the Vale of Eden and the land between coast and mountains south of St Bees on the flanks of the Furness Fells. They appear in some degree to have assimilated or been assimilated by the neolithic folk as few of the settlements are of pure Bronze Age type. The basis of their life was hunting combined with a pastoral dependence upon sheep and cattle and the cultivation of grain in small plots of ground cleared on the edge of the forest and on the rich valley soils. The ruling caste and their descendants might well demand tribute from the rest, but all the time there was a steady integration into a single population.

This fusion of Neolithic and Bronze Age people progressed steadily to form what we might with justification regard as the emergence of a basic Lakeland 'native' stock. The post-glacial climate was undergoing changes, and after a warm dry spell about 500 B.C. it again turned colder and wetter. Increasing populations on the continent of Europe encouraged further westward migrations of a people who, besides farming, had become miners of iron and salt and also workers of iron. Their ornaments, brooches, mirrors, horse-trappings (for they were great breeders and users of horses) and enamelling are of superb artistic craft, the gems of all our museums. Many arrived in our country as travelling tinkers and small trading craftsmen finding work and livelihood peaceably among the natives. They brought with them also their cultural ideas and habits of organisation, to which we have given the name Celtic. As in the Pennine Dales, a considerable Celtic or Iron Age element created the confederacy of the Brigantes, ruled by a king or queen and having a gold coinage and sufficient military and civil organisation to make them a 'nation', even if not a very clearly defined one. This confederacy occupied much of the Pennines and Lake District.

Because of the cold wet climate the majority of the Iron Age settlements were made on the well-drained limestone soils of the peripheral areas and on the very gravelly glacial deposits in the valleys and on the lower fells. Many of these settlements are still to be seen by the interested visitor. It was the Brigantes who were in possession of the Lake District when the arrogant invasion of the Roman armies attempted to seize and subjugate the whole British people.

The commonest Celtic unit in the organised society was the family group of four generations, which often kept their own separate grouping of huts, crofts, cattle pounds and pasture as a distinct settlement. In the broader social structure there was something approaching a class system. The Celts venerated poets and bards, artistic craftsmen, and medicine men: these last were the Druids, who also knew and practised the law. A middle class was made up of the independent farmers, both those owning and those renting their land, and traders. At the bottom of the scale were the labourers and slaves.

The Roman Interlude

The Romans can be regarded as creating an interlude in the development of Lakeland's character, but their lasting influence was small in comparison with that of other peoples who have contributed to the Lakeland stock. Roman armies invaded Britain in 43 A.D. and spread their conquest quickly over the south and midlands, but their conquest of the north was by no means easy. The Roman general Agricola did not complete his attacks on Wales until 78 A.D., and then had to tackle the problem of the Brigantes on the Pennines, in the Lake District and on the Scottish Border. Chester became an important Roman fort in a strategic position, and from there in about 79 A.D. an advance was made to the north and a small fort was established at Watercrook just south of Kendal in 90 A.D. As a means to subdue the Brigantes a main road to the north was constructed on the east side of the Pennines and another on the west side up to Ambleside and from there across the heart of the Lake District by the Hard Knott Pass to Ravenglass on the west coast. A fort was established near the summit of the pass. Another road was built north from Ribchester by the Lune and Eden valleys to Carlisle. In 122 to 130 A.D. the emperor Hadrian completed his Wall from Wallsend on the Tyne estuary to Bowness on Solway. This separated the Brigantes from support that might have come from the Picts of Scotland.

The Romans enslaved many Celts as serfs, and from the whole countryside demanded levies of food for their garrisons and for sending to other parts of the empire. These demands intensified the farming and encouraged the extension of land under cultivation. The Romans contributed an improved form of plough and their skill in draining techniques was of considerable benefit. The Celts, with their intensive sheep breeding and husbandry, had a large trade in wool, woollen cloth, and particularly in large woollen cloaks that were an important article of trade in exchange for pottery and other goods. There was some commercial contact between Romans and Britons, but on the whole the Romans remained 'foreigners' and were never assimilated. Some use was made of their roads after their withdrawal in about 410 A.D.; but the road over High Street, which is rather problematically credited to the Romans, was in the thirteenth century known as Brettestrete, the Britons' road.

In one sphere the Romans did have influence, perhaps not widespread or very obvious. This was in religion. Some of the Roman army had contacted Christians in Rome during the early days of the proscription of the Christian religion; some of the Druids learned of this and, with their own interest in religious thinking, must have discussed Christian beliefs with them in secret before the declaration of Christianity as the official state religion in 333 A.D. All this helped the work and contributed to the development of the Celtic church during the later years of the fourth century.

Post Roman—Fifth Century to Norman Conquest

The population that was slowly becoming 'native' to the Lake District must have greeted the withdrawal of the Roman armies with considerable relief. The Celtic Britons soon established a north-western kingdom of Rheged, which extended from the Solway to the Ribble and was part of a larger confederacy of the Cymry (Celts) that stretched southward from the Clyde to include North Wales. At one time there was a king, Urien, by some said to have been born at Pendragon Castle in Mallerstang. This area became part of the Scottish kingdom of Strathclyde which was to last until the tenth century. An abundance of Celtic place and river-names remain from that time: examples among many are the rivers Derwent, Ehen, Calder, Esk and others, hills like

Blencathra, place-names Penruddock and Glenderamakin and the towns Carlisle and Penrith.

Some traces of the legendary lore so characteristic of the superstitions of the Celts and of Scandinavia have persisted even to recent times. Some of the great stone circles, though not in fact of Celtic origin, are still spoken of as Druid Circles. The great monoliths on a Penrith grave are said to mark the resting place of the Celtic giant Tarquin and not far away is the location of the Giant of Eamont Bridge. Eveling, the king of the Celtic fairies, and his daughter Modron, later written as Morgan La Fee, were, until quite lately, believed to haunt the Roman ruins at Ravenglass. A 'Barguest' (a large ghostly dog) was, within a few generations back, exorcised at Beetham, and many of his tribe, by some called 'Padfoot', were well known and feared over much of the Lake District. Besides Barguest there were other ghostly prognosticators: the Seven Whistlers, Gabriel's Hounds and Gabble Ratchets, which may have had Celtic or Norse origins but remained a living tradition in northern parts until well into the nineteenth century. The Whistlers had been condemned by the Anglian scholar-cleric Alcuin, and all these apparations were known to Wordsworth and used in one of his sonnets.

> *Rich are his walks with supernatural cheer . . .*
> *He the seven birds hath seen, that never part,*
> *Seen the SEVEN WHISTLERS in their nightly rounds,*
> *And counted them: and often times will start —*
> *For overhead are sweeping GABRIEL's HOUNDS*
> *Doomed, with their impious Lord, the flying Hart*
> *To chase for ever, on aerial grounds!*

I have listened to both over the Pennine moors but only very rarely on the Lake District fells during an occasional New Year holiday visit. The Seven Whistlers are identifiable as a group of curlew. The Gabriel Hounds are noisier with a sound like a bunch of hounds or beagles scurrying by. Yarrell, the great naturalist, identifies them as bean geese from Scotland and Scandinavia on their winter move to the south and making their dog-like noise. On hearing all are taken as portents of a death somewhere in the neighbourhood. Gabble Ratchet is only a local corruption of Gabriel Hound.

A more valuable inheritance from the Celts was the support given to the spread of Christianity by the Celtic church and its missionaries in the fourth, fifth and sixth centuries. A very active teacher was Kentigern, the first bishop of Strathclyde, who came down from Glasgow to the Lake District on his way to Wales in about 550 A.D. He is said to have planted a cross and preached to large crowds at Great Crosthwaite, where again he preached in 573 A.D. and established a church. On his first journey he founded the church at Aspatria, and later others at Caldbeck, Mungrisdale, Grinsdale, Castle Sowerby, Bromfield and Irthington, besides preaching to large crowds at prominent places like the Druid Circle at Castlerigg near Keswick. He was throughout his life a noted ascetic, popularly reported to sleep in a stone coffin-like trough. Saint Bridget is associated with St Bees and the north-western part of the Lake District, and before his death Cuthbert of Lindisfarne made the effort to visit Carlisle where he met his old friend Hereberit, the hermit of Derwentwater, remembered now on St Herbert's Isle. Saint Patrick and Saint Columba also had brief contacts with the Lake District.

While the Celtic church was helping to christianise the Lake District and the north, and Roman missionaries were busy in the south and east, the leaders of another invasion had already appeared. The Angles and the Danes, Scandinavian peoples from the lowlands around the Baltic, had made raids on the east coasts of Britain, bringing massacre and conquest to much of the eastern and midland areas and destroying villages and churches alike. As the Angles moved to the north they seized the two small kingdoms that were north of the Humber, Deira and Bernicis, which later united to become Northumbria under King Aethelfrith; and in 615 A.D. Aethelfrith at the battle of Chester separated Cumbria from Wales and the Angles began their steady western expansion into Cumbria.

The Anglian folk were arable and dairy farmers, well organised in small village communities of about ten families. The houses and farm buildings, of timber, ranged round a central space, the 'green', and were surrounded by a timber palisade enclosing small crofts. There were two or three ploughing fields, then pasture and woodland. Outside that was the waste. The Angles created the greater number of the villages in the lowland Lakeland areas. They undertook much clearing of forest in order to expand their arable fields, and they built many churches. At many of these, finely carved stone crosses were erected in the graveyard as memorials or as preaching crosses, and what remains of these today are among the most admired of ancient monuments. One of the finest is in the churchyard at Gosforth in lower Eskdale, made in the seventh century. The general pattern of farm life in the lower country remained true for a thousand years to its Anglian pattern, with the cultivated land encircling the village, which later became the manor.

Into this predominantly Anglian countryside came another people with a way of life and a culture that were to become a powerful and permanent element giving to the true Cumbrian some of the character that distinguishes him from all other northern folk. These people were the Norse-Irish, Vikings in origin, who after extensive raiding on the east coast progressed by the north and west coasts of Scotland to the conquest of much of Ireland. There they settled and absorbed much of the Irish Celtic culture, blending it with strong Norse traditions. By way of the Isle of Man they came to the Lancashire and South Cumbrian coast and found settlement as neighbours to the Anglian farmers on the abundant uplands and valley heads that the Angles had left unused. The Norsemen were sheep-farmers looking for upland pasturage, even mountain pasture, resembling their traditional homeland. Such country to the Angles had been merely 'the Waste'. Following their tradition of 'transhumance' the Norsemen made their main settlements in the mid and upper valleys but in the summer months moved the family to be with their sheep and a few cattle in summer shielings given names ending in -erg and -saetre. The normal pattern of Norse settlement was single and isolated farms, or the occasional tiny group of two or three huts belonging to one extended family. These dwellings were generally in the 'out waste' of an Anglian parish with its church in the village. In time the Norse would have their own small church somewhere within reach of the scattered settlers, and at some of these churches in the tenth and eleventh centuries they adapted the memorial cross by giving it a wheel head and finer and more intricately patterned carvings often with human and animal figures. Their gravestones were often of the 'hog back' type, that is in the form of a house with a bear hugging each gable. Several of these have survived and, like Norse crosses, may be seen in a number of places.

The tallish shepherd of the hills today carries the physical features of the ancestral Norseman, and his quiet almost silent manners, isolation and sturdy independence are a part of his inheritance. The Norse Settlers continued to arrive right into the twelfth century, becoming the dominant element in the valleys and fells of the central dome.

The Norman Invasion

During the eleventh century the Norman armies invaded Britain, conquering the native British at the battle of Hastings in 1066 and in the following years spreading their conquest over most of the country. Cumbria, however, still remained a part of Strathclyde, and Scotland claimed the Lake District. After the defeat of Dunmail, the last king of Cumbria, in 945 A.D. by Edmund of Northumbria, Cumbria had been given to Malcolm king of the Scots and it remained with him until 1032. Cumbria, with a strong Scots-Norse element, was not included in the Normans' Domesday survey of their England, and it was divided not into counties but into baronies. The Normans did not come to Cumbria until 1092 when William Rufus entered Carlisle and made it a Norman town. It was then that many Flemings were brought over by the Normans and settled in the northern parts around the city, but they had little permanent effect on the local populations. To subdue the natives and to offer some defence against the Scots many castles were built in the peripheral areas: among them were Carlisle, Kendal, Egremont and Beckermet, all of motte and bailey, timber built with a timber stockade. Some of them, like Kendal and Appleby, were soon replaced by larger stone castles, the buildings or ruins that we see today.

The Norman invaders were military adventurers intent on conquest and plunder, a non-productive ruling aristocracy with very little to give and everything to take. The feudal system, with its legal theft of the community-owned land of Britain and its legal vesting of all property in the king, enabled him to reward his favourites with huge gifts in return for military service — vast tracts of land and numbers of manors and whole villages with their populations. We are still burdened with the inheritors of many of these stolen gifts. The Norman feudal aristocracy gave their military support to the crown but were parasitic on the peasantry. Fortunately they had no share in the character-making of the people or on native culture, except perhaps to induce a rebellious strain that has served the northerner well in several risings to defend or secure his rights.

The Norman Conquest was accomplished by massacre and pillage on a ferocious and unprecedented scale. Whole villages with their populations were burned and wide areas devastated and laid to waste by a vicious madman, William Rufus, brother in type and spirit to Hitler. None the less the second and later generations of Norman barons in the course of securing benefit for themselves inadvertently secured some benefit for Cumbria, a benefit in which the peasants, or at least some of them, might share. The maintenance of large garrisons and a great body of servants and retainers at and around the castles demanded a constant inflow of food stocks that included much that could not be supplied by levy on the local estate. For example wines and luxury foods were in great demand. To secure these things traders had to be brought in from distant places, and to accommodate them a market was established at the castle gates with proper regulation and protection. To these markets the local people had access. By the twelfth and thirteenth centuries they had been granted royal charters and most castle towns became and still are important market towns.

The greatest fear in the religion of these Dark Ages and in the feudal church was not of God but of Hell and Purgatory. The Church allowed one to buy one's soul out of these undesirable places, at a price. Founding a church or endowing a chantry with a priest to offer continuous prayer for a particular soul, usually a parent or other relation, could in proper scale shorten a stay in Purgatory. A more generous gift, a vast expanse of wooded waste (not usually from the best part of one's estate) given to found a monastery, would almost certainly purchase the surety of eventual heaven. It was in the twelfth century that most of our monasteries were founded and the continuance of these hopes and fears brought extension and enrichment of estates and endowments.

The monasteries with their building programmes brought together large companies of lay brethren, craftsmen of all kinds, workers in stone, wood, metals and textiles, architects and planners. On their estates agricultural methods were improved and better exploitation of their resources was explored and carried through. Among the ideas for expansion the one most commonly adopted was sheep rearing and a great wool trade; but in Furness iron mining and making was developed and, after the monastery had gone, became a great and important industry. Although the monks were not always good landlords, life on their estates was in some ways generally better than on the land of a feudal baron. This, however, is a subject to which an abundant and growing literature has been devoted, so this brief reminder will be sufficient for our purpose.

Cumbria and the Borderers

To the Lake District as it settled down in the centuries after the Conquest, Scotland proved a far from kindly neighbour. During the twelfth and thirteenth centuries some improvements in agriculture had been made on the very extensive monastic sites and in some areas poor land had been drained and parts of the forest cleared. Carlisle had been made a strong military post from which the attempt could be made to impose some rule on the Scots. This was resisted and counter-attacks became frequent, with a siege of Carlisle in 1296 and the burning of Lanercost Priory. The whole Border was subject to raids. In 1306 Robert Bruce became king of the Scots and, not long after, won success at Bannockburn. In 1314 Brough and Appleby were destroyed by raiders who had come through Northumberland and across the Pennines by way of Stainmore.

The Scots raids continued with increasing frequency and ferocity, and this led those farmers who had the means to build for themselves a new kind of defensive dwelling, the tower-houses or 'pele towers' that are unique to the north and are more numerously preserved in Cumbria than anywhere else. A typical pele tower is a square three-storeyed tower of extra-strong stone construction. Walls may be from four or five to ten feet thick, with few very small windows and a strong defensible entrance at ground or first floor level. The vaulted ground floor could accommodate stock in an emergency. The first floor, above the stone vault, was kitchen and living place for servants and the second floor was living and sleeping space for the master's family. There was access to the roof, which was a regular look-out post. The pele stood within a palisaded area, the barnkiln, and in this too stock could be kept in time of danger. The peles that remain today are objects of great interest and deserve better preservation than is afforded to many of them. Most have seventeenth century houses built against them now, and the tower is only used for casual store or for stock. They are most numerous in the north-east along the Border country, along the whole Vale of Eden and down the west coast. The valleys of the central dome are free of them, for there, on any alarm, the stock could be driven up into the fells. By the fifteenth century the Scottish raids had virtually ceased except for small cattle-raids both ways across the border.

The real successors to the Border raiders were the cattle drovers of the seventeenth and eighteenth centuries who brought vast numbers of Highland cattle down to the English market even as far south as Smithfield. They gave little trouble to the Lake District, which had few roads except from Carlisle down the Vale of Eden and then by the Lune Valley into Lancashire. Most of the drove roads avoid all towns and as far as possible keep to the wilder summits of the Pennines where along many of them there are grassy resting places where stock could rest and feed. The many drove roads are highly appreciated today by the increasing number of ramblers who are discovering them afresh.

Rural Life

For much of the Lake District the century 1650 to 1750 could be regarded as almost revolutionary, a transition from life patterns that were in many ways a continuance of earlier centuries to those more characteristic of the modern world. Heavy industries were being established and developed, timber houses and buildings were being replaced by stone, pony tracks were being enlarged into, or superseded by, roads for wheeled vehicles and there were many changes in marketing methods. On arable farms traditional cropping was being replaced by crop rotations. In the central fells and valleys, however, where sheep farming was still dominant, there were still some havens of old custom, and in the isolated farms and hamlets, though the living was hard, this did not preclude a high quality of life.

The most noticeable change in the fell area was the replacement of timber hovels by stone cottages on a more commodious plan, and a close network of rough-built stone walls spread over and embraced the upper valleys, dividing up common fields and parts of the common pasture into numerous small crofts.

Turning from landscape to people, we must go back to the ending of the monasteries and to the break-up of their great estates. A feature of the monastic system already mentioned was the founding of many chantries both within the monasteries and in the many outlying 'chapels' that they served on their estates. At the dissolution of the monasteries the greater part of the monastic estates were sold, some to local gentry and many to merchant speculators who quickly resold them for profit. A few scholars like Erasmus and ecclesiastics like Latimer hoped that the monastic wealth would be used to endow schools and universities, but the king's financial embarrassment prevented most of these ideas from being implemented. There is little doubt, however, that monastic schools had left some strong tradition of learning among the gentry and those who before long became the 'statesmen' or small landowners. Within a generation or two following the end of the monasteries some of these men, becoming wealthy and feeling the need for educational provision for their sons and for their class, founded many small grammar schools. By the end of the eighteenth century there were forty-six such schools in the Lakeland area, most of them founded during the sixteenth century. At these schools the classics, particularly Latin with some Greek reading and writing, were the main part of the curriculum together with some simple arithmetic. Many schools taught, as a special subject, mathematics of a high standard. Many schools were endowed with scholarships that sent a steady stream of students to the colleges of Oxford and Cambridge.

Throughout the area there were also smaller parish schools, often taught by the curate or parson in the church. In these the teaching was less of classics and, after the basic reading and writing, more of practical 'accounts and mensuration' with sometimes a little botany and farm science. From the Lakeland schools have come several remarkable men, and in the seventeenth and eighteenth centuries travellers into remote valleys were often surprised to find small farmers and other individuals with an unexpected level of education. Mathematics and natural philosophy were by no means unknown and many a labourer or small farmer could make an efficient and very knowledgeable guide to the botany of his own area. It was a local dalesman, John Wilson, who in 1744, following John Ray's *Synopsis methodica stirpium britannicarum* (3rd edition 1724), published *A Synopsis of British Plants in Mr Ray's Method,* a classic of early botany that became the treasured text-book of many dalesmen. Among many botanists coming from the dales the most remarkable must be John Gough, born in Kendal in 1757 and blind from his second year. His father was Thomas Gough, one of the Quaker community of Wyresdale in Lancashire, who did everything in his power to educate John and help him overcome his disability. In this he was remarkably successful. John took to botany as a child, having the help and care of many local Quakers. He went to the Quaker school, later Stramongate, in Kendal and there George Bewley, the headmaster, introduced him to Wilson's *Synopsis* and to the *Flora Anglica* (1762) of William Hudson, another Kendal Friend. As he grew up Gough became an arbiter on most botanical questions not only for the north of England flora but over much of Europe. He was a valued friend of Wordsworth, the teacher of Dalton and correspondent of William Withering whose *A botanical arrangement of all vegetables naturally growing in Great Britain* (1776) is another landmark in British botany.

In their humble way the schools produced many scientists who, in the importance of their contribution to the culture of the area and to the country at large, deserve to rank with the well-publicised poets and writers of the district. Dalton and Gough were by no means alone in this. In 1709 Thomas Robinson, parson of Ousby though not Dales-born, produced one of the first books on the Lake District, his *Essay towards a Natural History of Westmorland and Cumberland,* which gave us the first rational account of 'their several Mineral and Surface Productions'. He discussed the various mineral fields and put forward an acceptable theory of the origin and extent of mineral veins. In the true spirit and habit of his time he added an appendix of equal length, 118 pages, *A Vindication of the Philosophical and Theological Paraphrase of the Mosaic System of the Creation,* and thus justified his position as a priest. He was followed by Jonathan Otley (1766-1856), born in Keswick, who in 1820 published in the *Lonsdale Magazine* the first account of the subdivision of the rocks of the Lake District, a work that remains a minor classic and was highly valued by Adam Sedgwick in his work on the area. A man of very different character was Richard Watson (1737-1816), who became rector of Ousby and later, as Bishop of Llandaff, managed to hold his bishop's see for very many years without visiting it more than once. His time was spent in scientific experiment and he produced four volumes of *Chemical Essays* 1781-1786, which contain much pioneer work on metallurgy with the vastly important suggestion that long flues should be used for the condensation of the poisonous fumes emitted by lead smelting furnaces, a practice that soon came into use in almost every field where lead ores were smelted.

Many non-conformists, debarred by the Test Acts from the older universities, went to the medical schools of Edinburgh and Leyden and returned to their home district and a life of service as doctors. William Woodville, born in Cockermouth in 1752, graduated at Edinburgh in 1773 and made a special study of smallpox and also of the use of herbs in medicine. His great *Medical Botany* was published in three volumes in

1790, 1792 and 1793. He was physician to the Middlesex Dispensary and Small Pox Hospital and, after several years there, founded the St Pancras Small Pox Hospital in 1791, remaining there as physician until his own death from smallpox in 1805. He was a great supporter of Jenner in his fight for innoculation. These are only a few of the many Lakeland scientists who became known to the wider scientific world.

In the richer agricultural lowlands of the north, east and south-east the life-style and authority of the 'statesman' was of increasing wealth and estate and he was an employer of much wage-labour as in the rest of agricultural Britain; while on the estates and round the farms the life of the labourer and his family was little different from that of the labouring poor in most of the country. In the valleys of the Lake District mountain area, however, there was a notable difference. There, population was thinner and based on sheep-farming, and there were fewer statesmen or larger estates. The scatter of farms were grouped in the valleys in communities that only by courtesy could be called hamlets. These were sufficiently cohesive to have a rich life of their own. The mountain topography, with an almost entire lack of transport except on foot or by pack-pony on ways that crossed high passes, some at heights around two thousand feet above sea level, made for isolation of the valleys as quite separate, self-contained communities. This self-containment caused and was in turn increased by marriages being mostly confined to those between members of the same community.

Among these small scattered communities at the valley heads there are a few small churches, mainly sixteenth century replacements in stone of very early chapels of ease; and at these until recent times the living was very small, sometimes only a few pounds and usually not more than fifty pounds even in a 'good' living. The parson was one of the working people of the area. An eighteenth-century parson, typical of several, was Robert Watson of the Duddon valley from 1736 to 1802. His glebe was two acres; and on this and on some extra land that by hard labour he reclaimed from the waste he kept two cows. On the fell pastures he had a small flock of sheep from which he raised wool that he combed in his small cottage and spun in his church. There he had two wheels that he used, while teaching children of the area who had no other school. His school did not meet in winter as the long walk that many of the children had to make would be dangerous or impossible in bad weather. The wool provided all the clothes for his family, and any surplus was accumulated and then carried on a pack-pony to market at a distant town, probably Ulverston. In bad weather he provided bowls of hot soup for his parishioners who had walked long distances over the fells to church. The broth was the water in which he had boiled his weekly joint of dried mutton. This gave rise to the saying 'It's hot and wet like Seathwaite broth'. He also sold home-brewed beer after the service, he being the only brewer in the valley.

In common with all the country parsons he made wills and wrote letters for most of his flock. At all times he was an extra hand to be hired for farm work. For his care and kindness he was greatly loved.

Watson was typical of the small 'statesman' farmer, with his own house and independence. The more prosperous of these have left us the fine 'statesman' houses from the seventeenth and eighteenth centuries, so much admired today. The eighteenth century was a time of relative prosperity with a noticeable growth in the rural population and commensurate expansion in the wool trade. This was reflected in the growth of Kendal as the virtual centre and main market of this trade, with a large carrying organisation that took Kendal wool and Kendal Green woollen cloth to many parts of the country, even as far as the midlands and the south. The principal contact between the mountain valleys and the outside world was the necessary journey to such a market town, accomplished on horseback with attendant pack-pony carrying the wool crop and, when available, surplus butter and eggs and maybe honey. The market-going farmer on occasion took his wife on pillion behind him.

An equally valued link not only with the outside world but with neighbouring valleys was a group of itinerants, not highly placed in the social scale but invaluable to the community: the pedlar, the tinker and the tailor. Each had his regular rounds, each was an expected and welcome visitor. The arrival of the pedlar with his staggeringly sized pack at one farm, possibly a customary haven, was the signal for the gathering of women from the whole community while the pedlar was having bite and sup, the duly appreciated hospitality. The event that all awaited was the opening of the pedlar's pack, containing the common haberdashery, needles and pins, threads and tapes and all the little daily necessities of the housewife, with ribbons and laces, perhaps handkerchiefs, and small articles of clothing that might have a suggestion of fashion about them. A few dress lengths of new design and better materials were always popular, but most eagerly sought of all was the news that the pedlar brought not only from the markets but, even more valued, of neighbours and relatives seen and talked with in the course of his round. On some occasions the pedlar broke his journey by staying overnight at a house, and the evening was spent by a fine gathering round the fireside with more news received and messages given, all leavened with songs, tales and legend.

The tinkers were different in many ways. They were craftsmen, skilled in and exercising a 'mystery' craft, often members of a gypsy family. They could not bring caravans into the mountain valleys, but many travelled with a light cart and a pony, of the popular dappled and distinctive breed. The tinker was supplementary to the blacksmith, sharing some of his skills but working in lighter sheet metals. He repaired and even made the numerous smaller objects of kitchen, dairy and farm, and could be useful in many ways. He was not as intimate to the family as was the pedlar, but none the less was another link with the outside world.

The tailor was a rarer visitor but stayed some time, a few days to a few weeks, living in the family and working for it as well as bringing with him welcome news not only of neighbours where he had worked but of fashions and happenings from a wider world. The pedlar and the market might have provided some finer cloth or dress goods and a few families grew and spun flax for linens, all accumulated for the tailor's visit; but most of the clothes needed would be made up from home-grown wool. Some houses had a handloom perhaps in the bedroom or some other nook of the house where at times the man could weave up some of the yarn into a long-wearing cloth suitable for his rough work. But in any case this part of the tailor's material was the product of an elaborate series of domestic operations.

Each family had its sheep, some few and some many, and the care of them was regulated by fixed traditional positions on the shepherds' calendar. When winter has been survived and lambing, with its extra cares, has been brought to a satisfactory conclusion, other jobs loom ahead. Because of the scattered nature of the settlements, it has always been custom and necessity to turn some of these into occasions when the farmers give and receive co-operative help and these have become the community's chief social events. Sheep washing, sauving and shearing are such events, when day by day in arranged order farmers gather at stated farms to make a mass attack on the work in hand while the womenfolk hold a session of gossiping, cooking and baking to feed the dozen or so workers. These are occasions when boys are welcome in small jobs and so get their training in the whole tradition of sheep management. Many a boy of ten or twelve would surprise a lowland farmer by his skill in sheep handling. The boys are almost as essential to the working company as are the dogs. On completion of the operation, in which there is some competition for speed and quality of work, each gathering is closed on the last evening with a great supper and a dance that traditionally continues through most of the night.

Though the bulk of the wool crop would be carried by pack-horse to one of the wool markets and the proceeds eagerly counted as part of the year's cash income, a portion would be chosen and set aside for home use. This must be scoured, carded and, in innumerable snatched intervals of household duties and at the fireside gathering in the evening, with the spinning wheel always handy, would be spun into yarns of more than one grade. This is the universal occupation of the mountain valleys, a central feature of life that is a gentle and peacefully unifying family medium. These evening gatherings have taken a prominent place in rural legends through the literary prominence given to them by William and Mary Howitt and by Southey. Adam Sedgwick of Dent has left us the warmest and most intimate account of them as he experienced them in his boyhood at his home. Adam, like his home dale of Dent, is a permanent link between Lake District and Pennines. Look from the hills above Dent at sunset and to the west you see the Howgill Fells and beyond them the Lake District hills glowing with evening light, all part of one geological mass. Look east and south-east at dawn and you see the Yorkshire Dales with their fells catching the sun's first rays and composing a different country of beckoning shadowy dales. It would be hard to say to which country Dentdale belongs. In fact it partakes of both, with all the allure of each, and Adam Sedgwick has spoken for both of them.

Some of us as children revelled in grandmother's memories of her girlhood years, who from her own grandmother had gathered the recollections of such fireside evenings. From that grandmother of an older generation came tales of ghosts, legends of the 'little people', the news of how Hob Thrush had been playing tricks at a local farm or how a neighbour, returning from market and no doubt well primed, had seen Guytrash. Traditional songs enlivened some evenings and on some specially remembered occasions the schoolmaster had been invited in to read something of his own choice to busy spinners and knitters. The men often took advantage of the candle and fire-light to prepare new hafts for tools, do some wood-carving (a legacy from Norse ancestry) and repair wooden vessels. It was here that a young man would carve a knitting sheath for his true love, for some a simple practical sheath that took as much labour as went with greater skill to carve the highly patterned example. The basic and enduring pattern was the same, and it did not change in substance nor did the fashion and custom die out until modern times.

Much of this simple co-operative character is still basic among the Lakeland folk. It is not displayed in information centres or in the literature, nor is it obvious, but it is there to be experienced by the genuine lover of the district.

Though life in the central valleys of Lakeland has for the most part continued until recent times on much the same course as in other of the more rural areas of Britain, there was one movement between the middle of the seventeenth and the middle of the eighteenth centuries that affected the people very deeply. About 1650 George Fox set out from his Leicestershire home to take his message to the people: that God spoke directly to his people without the intermediacy of priest or church and that every man had that of God within himself that was capable of wholly guiding his life if that 'inward light' was seen and followed. He travelled through Yorkshire, holding many meetings at which he preached to crowds, and came in 1652 to Pendle Hill and Barley on the borders of Lancashire and Yorkshire. Here, helped by talk with folk on his way, he had a perception that there was a people in the northern parts, in Westmorland and parts of Yorkshire, who were ripe for his message. These were people of Swaledale, of the dales around Sedbergh and around Preston Patrick in Westmorland. Discontented with Anglican liturgy and theology, they had been gathering under leaders to meet together in small groups, mostly in silence, to seek the guidance of the holy spirit, the 'inward light' of Fox, to be shown a more acceptable way of life and of religion. They called themselves Seekers. Fox made his way to them in the weeks before Whit in 1652, and after meeting with many of them preached to a great crowd in and around Sedbergh churchyard. In spite of much opposition he convinced many by his message. A meeting followed at Firbank Chapel, when Fox preached outside it on the fellside of the Howgills, and a few years later he preached again at a general meeting of Seekers at Preston Patrick. Many were convinced at these meetings, and the Society of Friends, 'in scorn called Quakers', there had its beginnings. Meetings gathered and were settled in many places, at Swarthmoor near Ulverston, at Kendal, Grayrigg, Underbarrow and Crook. In the next few years meetings were established over most of the Lake District and particularly in the central mountain valleys the Quaker message proved acceptable so that some valleys became almost entirely Quaker and the town of Kendal was spoken of before long as Quaker Kendal.

The quiet sincerity and simplicity of the Quakers harmonised well with the basic character of the valley folk. The early enthusiasm of the Quaker convincement, which established the Westmorland-Yorkshire corner of the Lake District as the birthplace and home of Quakerism, is emphasised in George Fox's *Journal* where, describing the earliest years of the movement, he says: 'And so when the churches were settled in the north, the Lord had raised up many and sent forth many into his vineyard to preach his everlasting Gospel, as Francis Howgill and Edward Burrough to London, John Camm and John Audland to Bristol through the countries, Richard Hubberthorne and

George Whitehead towards Norwich, and Thomas Holme into Wales, a matter of seventy ministers did the Lord raise up and send abroad out of the north countries.' These in later Quaker literature became known (despite George's count of seventy) as The Valiant Sixty.

Men and women took the Quaker message to many parts of the world in spite of persecution. Howgill, Burrough, and Hubberthorne all died in prison. Mary Fisher, a Yorkshire servant girl, became convinced and with her companion, Elizabeth Williams, went to Cambridge in 1653 where they were arrested, stripped and scourged for preaching. Later Mary went along to speak to the Grand Turk in Adrianople, doing much of the journey on foot. She had a long session with him, speaking and preaching to him and an assembly of his ministers and others. Though persecution was extreme the northern people accepted it without giving up their mission. A report of 1658 says that 'the numbers of all the said sufferers come to hand amount to 12,316 in this country, many in prison and many distrained of all their goods'. In Britain the centre of the new Society of Friends was Swarthmoor Hall, Ulverston, the home of Judge Fell who, though he never joined the Friends, was very sympathetic to them, and all his family became Quakers. Swarthmoor Hall today is almost a place of pilgrimage for Quakers from all parts of the world.

The Coming of Industry

It was in the sixteenth and seventeenth centuries that great changes were brought about in the agriculture and industries of the Lake District, changes that affected the lives of the inhabitants in very many ways. Until then the lowland farmers had largely preserved the Anglian methods and customs, while the sheep farmers on the high fells and in the mountain valleys still followed the pattern set in the tenth century by the Norsemen who had themselves accepted from their Celtic predecessors some of their practices as well as their system of numbering. Local industry, too, had a venerable ancestry. Among the excavated debris from many Iron Age village sites, such as those on Birkrigg, have been found slags from iron making and working. The Celtic 'tinkers' may have formed a special craft group carrying their 'mystery' of iron making from settlement to settlement among their people, and their trade was continued and encouraged in the Dark Ages following the Roman occupation. In Furness, on the limestone peripheral to the Lake District, Furness Abbey — following a common Cistercian habit and in at least three areas, Orgrave, Elliscales and Marton — had granted leases for mining iron ore and for washing and dressing it. This was in the early years of the thirteenth century. Way-leaves were granted for the dressed ore to be carried by pack ponies, by sledge or even by primitive cart to the 'bloomeries' in areas where charcoal was being made and was available in sufficient quantity for iron making. The 'bloomery' or bowl furnace used charcoal many times the weight of the iron ore in making iron, and so it was easier to take the ore to the charcoal than to bring charcoal to the ore. The carriers' animals were given the right to feed along their ways and to stop overnight at places called stances along their regular route. A few stances, embanked or lightly walled areas of good grass with a spring of fresh water, can still be recognised by the knowledgeable visitor.

Similar leases to these had been granted by Conishead Priory and on the northern border of the limestone by Holme Cultram. There must have been quite a sizeable body of miners, washers and carriers concerned with the ore trade as well as the smelters whom they served. These many people formed an industry-based close-knit community within the general mass of the farming based peasantry. In the early mines of the thirteenth to fifteenth centuries all the ore was got from open-cast trenches or from small quarry workings in the open air and so subject to the weather and the seasons. During a hard winter there could be little or no work at the mines and subsistence crafts in the shelter of the villages would not be easy to find; but it is likely that the duty of alms-giving, which was part of monastic discipline, would have been extended where practicable to some of these 'laid off' sufferers.

As already mentioned, the smelting part of iron-making was done in bloomeries near the forests and mosses where charcoal was made and peat was cut. The smelters were in close dependence on the colliers and peat cutters and so to a large extent their work was seasonal, though some attempt was made to accumulate stocks of fuel to see them over part of the winter. This also meant storing dressed ore, and both operations were matters of great difficulty. As on the Pennine ore fields, a form of smallholding was widely exercised. A small croft along with common rights could enable the miner to keep a pig, a few hens and geese and possibly a cow, if a little extra land was won from the waste. Some food could then be grown, perhaps hay and oats for winter feeding; and while the miner was at work wife and children could keep general watch on the animals and look after their feed and their young. The miner could make occasion for heavy digging and his family could plant a little kale. Spinning and knitting were a permanent household occupation and in the forest the charcoal burners often, while watching the coaling heap, could make baskets and besoms, turn trenchers, split hazels for the cooper's bindings and, above all, make hurdles with which it was essential to shelter the burning heaps from winds. A temporary hut for the burner was soon made and would last at least one season. This section of the population was not in the main village tradition and their dwellings were often those of squatters on the waste and on the fell sides, on the edge of cultivation and common village pastures. Their life was hard but it bred a sturdy independence. Some of the burners developed their woodland crafts into small industries that eventually might grow sufficiently to use a stream for water power and a stone building for accommodation. Cooperage, trencher and wood turning led, as textiles increased, to bobbin turning, and these occupations were the ancestors of the bobbin mills that have for some time been of interest to Lake District visitors.

These forest folk are a true part of the Lake District native population which expanded greatly in the sixteenth and seventeenth centuries but was almost to disappear in the twentieth. As the charcoaling and iron industries dwindled, together with the mining of both iron and lead, the workers migrated to the growing textile towns and in two or three generations became urbanised, now returning as visitors to look upon their original family homeland.

There had been in the Middle Ages another old occupation, not as extensive but just as skilled and venerable and, unlike charcoal and iron-making, still viable today — that which exploited the resources of slate. We have already noted the use of slate from Langdale and its surroundings as much as four thousand years ago. A few Roman buildings used slate as a roofing material and part of the monastic and castle buildings had slate roofs. While houses were almost everywhere timber-built and roofed with thatch and many castles used lead for roofing, slate was easily got in small quarries and unsplit rough slate was at an early date used for rough walling, though only on a very small and local scale. As a common building material slate came into great demand in the sixteenth century when the larger timber houses were being replaced in stone. Split slates were found to make excellent roofing and good floors. Slate quarrying, mining and dressing, if selective, then became a skilled profession and in a few areas high quality slate was mined and an industry grew that still persists. Much of the dressing is now done by power-driven machinery, but the old skill of slate-splitting is still used for the best slates and good splitters remain the aristocrats of the business. The use of power and the availability of saws armed with commercial diamond and artificial abrasives have now made it possible to produce sawn and polished slabs of almost any size from massive slate not of splitting quality. Today slate has become a fine architect's material, a substance with great ornamental variety and potential and a thriving export market.

The change from the small craftsman supplying local demand to the industry with wide external markets was so marked in the sixteenth century that we can take it as the opening of the modern age. The real change was seen when the new enterprise was expressly organised and directed to outside markets with the aim of making profits and securing returns for a few capital investors rather than of providing a livelihood for individual craftsmen. Wage labour on an extended scale was introduced by employers who were 'offcomers' or local gentry looking first and foremost to potential profits. Here in fact was the beginning of a capitalist economy aimed not at the needs of the local community but at profitable investment.

The first great manifestation of this change was the Elizabethan initiation of prospecting for exploitable mines of gold, silver, copper and lead in the Lake District. The exploration was carried out by German prospectors and metallurgists brought into the country between 1526 and 1531, at first to search Scotland. Later the Lake District was explored and some veins of copper ore were opened at Newlands near Keswick while other copper deposits were found near Caldbeck and Grasmere. In 1564, after wider prospecting and some small-scale mining, an association was formed by royal charter, the Governor, Assistants and Commonalty of the Mines Royal. For a time this was to have a great effect on life in the Lake District but its permanent effects were perhaps less than might have been expected. Miners were brought from the Tyrol and between 1564 and 1565 forty or more had arrived at Newcastle to be forwarded to Keswick. Stores of many kinds were sent regularly from Augsburg to Newcastle and then taken by pack horse trains to Keswick. The earlier knowledge of these mines had been with Thomas Thurland and Johann Steinberger, one of the early prospectors, and they had formed a small company to work a copper mine that in 1564 was transferred to Thurland and Daniel Hochstetter. Hochstetter was in fact the agent for a firm of bankers and merchants, Hans Langneuer and Company, who were amalgamated with the famous banking house of Fugger of Augsburg and were working extensive mines in Schwatz in the Tyrol. It was this group that invested capital in the Keswick mines and remained active partners with them for a few years. While some of the returns went to Langneuer and Co., some of the returns and rents were taken by the Crown towards their damnable business of armaments, much of the copper being used for making brass cannon.

Other miners were brought in succeeding years from Styrian mines. At first they were resented and attacked by local people but soon they were accepted and by 1567 fourteen of them had married local girls, an example followed by many others in the following years. Descendants of these marriages are still in the district, new Cumbrians of many generations. Most of the incomers were Lutherans, and this may have been a factor in the religious tolerance shown towards some of the Nonconformist settlements in the district.

The influence of the Germans was threefold: they introduced an advanced technology in the mines; the scale of their work was large and their smelting mills at Brigham near Keswick created a demand for charcoal that, with the heavy demands of timber for miners, denuded much of Skiddaw and Borrowdale of their forest cover, while large quantities of peat from Skiddaw and the various mosses were also taken. The factor of most human interest is the number of intermarriages, the descendants of which had some influence in the district. The scrupulous household pride, a few special dietary habits, Anglicised surnames and several pleasant customs, games and occasions are still to be detected by the careful and sympathetic student. The mining has now ceased but traces of it can still be seen in abundant sites on the fells.

In 1569 the Mines Royal brought ninety-two horse-loads of coal (stone coal) from Cockermouth to the smeltmill. This was an experiment, as the company's accounts include the entry 'Watchmen for several nights at the coal, to burn it. 1s 4d'. Deciding to use coal and to get it for themselves they make the entry 'Anthony Dediman, if he finds coalmines near Keswick, $1\frac{1}{2}$ miles from Smelthouses, to have £20 of which now £4 in hand and earnest money. £4.3.4.' Coal continued to be fetched from Cockermouth and Whitehaven, and this is evidence that coalpits were already at work near the west coast. The Mines Royal had been in treaty with Sir Patricius Curwen for land on which to make a wharf from which to export their copper to Dublin. Before the end of the century coal shafts had been sunk at several places, and harbours, from which coal could be shipped to Ireland, had been constructed at Maryport, Whitehaven and Workington and over 30,000 tons of coal had been exported. In the early seventeenth century Sir John Lowther was planning the new town of Workington. With the advent of blast furnaces for iron and steel-making, with shipping and with the backing of a broad belt of iron ore mines around Clifton and Egremont, this part of the Lake District became an industrial area of great importance. Through the eighteenth and nineteenth centuries it was as busy as any other heavy industrial area in Britain, and this development demanded great improvements in the infrastructure, with a nexus of new roads and later of railways that broke down the isolation of the Lake District as a whole. In the present century there has been a swift and effective decline, pits closed, furnaces blown out and works demolished. The west is now a derelict area seeking rejuvenation by some other means than coal and iron.

There has been one instance of industrial recovery in the north-west: the nuclear power station and nuclear waste recovery plant at Windscale, now renamed Sellafield. These installations are objects of fear and of some public opposition in spite of the employment that they have brought to several thousand men otherwise without work. The problems that they set concern both the general population and the planners and are becoming increasingly reflected in current politics. We shall return to them when we look to the future.

The Discovery of Lakeland

It is a sad reflection that the story of industry in the Lake District is largely one of the degradation and destruction of parts of a lovely coast and countryside, and also the exploitation of its people, for the sake of profit and the amassing of wealth by private families. Some relief from this history can be found if we briefly consider the 'discovery' of Lakeland by artists, poets and visitors, a movement that had its origins in the mid-eighteenth century. Earlier visitors had viewed the mountains with a large degree of terror and abhorrence. Defoe in 1724 and 1725 found the Lake country to be 'the wildest, most barren and frightful of any that I have passed over in England or even in Wales itself'. Among artists, however, and their client public a new mode of feeling was appearing, the search for and appreciation of 'the Picturesque'. That the picturesque need not be contrived and composed by the artist but was there to be found in nature was a new view asserted by critics like William Gilpin. His exposition of this discovery was made in the two volumes of his *Observations on the Mountains and Lakes of Cumberland and Westmorland* (1786), books that brought both artists and visitors to the area. A worsening of the political conditions on the Continent, and increasing difficulties for travellers there, persuaded some of the gentry to substitute, for their customary Continental Grand Tour, a Tour among the Lakes. Such a tour was facilitated by the increasing ease of movement along the proliferating turnpike roads by which the private coaches could penetrate parts of Lakeland that had previously been generally inaccessible. Carlisle and Kendal were centres from which already radiated sets of important roads linking all the market towns of the rural areas.

The accounts and journals of some of the early travellers show that, apart from the older coaching inns, the available accommodation was of the very poorest quality, insanitary, unclean and inadequate in almost every respect. The influx of visitors, their demands and the money that they brought into the area did much to bring about improvements in the living standards of many of the natives. By the middle of the nineteenth century many intolerable hovels had been replaced by new cottages, some roadside beer houses had become small inns and, in the towns, life was being geared to the demands of trade and the accommodation of tourists. It was then, too, that wealthy 'offcomers' began to settle in villa houses around Bowness, Windermere, Ambleside and other lakeside towns, which so began to expand into their modern form. In the Edwardian years the rapid increase in pressures from visitors and in the numbers of more extensive and fashionable houses with high rateable value, particularly in towns such as Keswick, Penrith, Appleby, Kendal and Ulverston, brought great benefit not only to commerce but to every household that could offer accommodation or services. The increasing prosperity was reflected in town improvements, in the removal of slum properties and in the provision of many community services.

A taste for exploring the fells on foot developed in the nineteenth century. The celebration of the beauties of Lakeland by the 'Lake poets' Wordsworth, Coleridge and Southey encouraged people to look for picturesque scenery, and the intimate contact with the landscape together with the physical enjoyment derived from this activity created a new respect for the mountains. The acme of this process was the arrival, about mid-century, of the first rock climbers, who appreciated the Lakeland crags as a challenge to new levels of skill and endurance. This new sport on the splendid rock faces offered in all parts of the central mountains quickly became an integral part of the life of the area, not only for visitors but for some Lakelanders like the Abraham brothers, who became climbing pioneers known throughout the world of the sport. Though climbing was only possible for a hardy minority, fell walking was becoming increasingly popular with many visitors and by the present century was being fostered as a normal recreation for thousands of visitors.

Other sports native to the area took on a new significance as attractions and entertainment for the tourists. Cumberland wrestling is famous, while hunting on foot and the closely related hound trailing are popular at most sports gatherings. The great crowds now attracted to the area pose a serious problem for the Lake District's planners, that of traffic control. Many of the car-borne visitors come only for the day and seek to penetrate far into the quieter areas by roads not designed for such traffic. This leads to pressure for road straightening and widening. The new road across the northern Lake District, from Penrith by Keswick to Cockermouth, is regarded by many as a desecration but by some as a pattern to be followed by other Lakeland roads.

Looking to the Future

If Lakeland is to be preserved and developed as a place where peace of mind and refreshment of spirit can be found by all, whether local inhabitants or visitors, then certain problems must be resolved.

Perhaps the simplest of these problems is the regeneration of the derelict industrial areas to the west. Much of the land indeed remains in its natural state and even today could be enjoyed by people seeking a quiet seaside holiday. Maryport, with its fine sands and easy access to the interior, has not been lost entirely, and the cliffs of St Bees Head rival in interest and beauty some parts of the inland scene. A beautiful coastline, a wide background of rich soil with many farms, and easy approaches to the finest mountains and lakes are an attraction to visitors and offer an encouraging start to recovery. Many minds today are engaged in earnest thought and are full of aspirations, hopes and dreams regarding the right outcome of the vital struggle that faces the people of this area. If only there could be inspired and courageous planning, this part might again in the years to come find itself one of the choicest elements in the beauty of a preserved Lake District. Similar aspirations are valid for the devastated tracts around Millom and Dalton and the industrial area of the south-western corner. No sensitive spirit can look on the Lake District and be content to write off the north-western and south-western portions because they have been desecrated by the greed of industrial exploitation.

The most intractable problem is that of Sellafield, for it has a moral as well as a physical dimension. The Russian disaster at Chernobyl, which spread a trailing cloud of threatened suffering and destruction over most of Europe, has heightened appreciation of the physical risks that Sellafield may pose for the Lake District and far beyond it. The public has indeed been assured of the impossibility of such accidents ever occurring at British nuclear stations, but to rely on this assurance is to join the sad believers in perpetual motion machines. No machinery as yet invented by man has ever totally escaped breakdown and eventual failure and abandonment, and no grouping of human beings has ever existed that has not been subject to human incompetence and miscalculation. The official records of the plant contain, moreover, a long catalogue of 'minor' failures and accidents, breakdowns and human errors that in public have been minimised or altogether withheld from the media. In addition we now have knowledge of the serious conditions created by the discharge of nuclear waste into the sea, poisoning the shore-line and harmfully affecting the Irish Sea as far as the Isle of Man.

The moral issues are two. The larger relates to the legitimacy of what is being done at Sellafield. Britain has become the reprocessing agent for many countries who, like the United States, have banned the operation in their own territories, transferring it to Britain and buying back the recovered plutonium. Japan and others are now following suit. Thus Britain is becoming the mainstay of the trade in plutonium for nuclear weapons that are being stockpiled for a war in which most of the life on earth would be eliminated. On the other hand the closing down of Sellafield would put out of work several thousand people for whom the plant provides the only job opportunity in the area, and the ending of one evil would generate another.

If only the money lavished on the nuclear industry could be diverted to the new technological research for a more rational means of drawing upon our coal resources than the present robbing of the thick seams to the exclusion of any possibility of working the thin seams at a later date. Research into the inexhaustible energy of tidal movement and into the recovery of energy from the sun's heat is at present starved of funds and could be properly financed. Money might also be found for retraining the nuclear industry's work-force for more reputable and more socially useful jobs. Unfortunately present economic policy is orientated towards increased profit and not to community needs. Yet somehow the fears generated by Sellafield must be removed if future generations are to be enabled to enjoy the lakes, mountains and coast of Lakeland as a haven of physical and spiritual renewal.

Lastly there are the general problems of control. The very popularity of the Lake District threatens to destroy the elements that make it popular. The two characteristics, other than the scenery, that most deserve to be preserved, are the peaceful quiet and the unpolluted air. Few places now remain that are beyond the noise of the internal combustion engine, and the noise is then accompanied by the poisonous exhaust fumes, which spread through the ambient air and destroy its purity. Wise planning can do much to prevent or mitigate these affronts, but however wise our planners may be they cannot solve this problem unaided. Planning demands some degree of control and cannot be effective without the willing acceptance, goodwill and co-operation of all. Every person who has a love for the area or who hopes to continue to enjoy its attractions must recognise that the beauties of a countryside are not to be had without some cost and sacrifice. The quiet of the lakes cannot be assured if the owners of powered speed-boats will not accept restriction and in some places prohibition. Car-drivers will have to accept limitations on their freedom to use any and every road at will. The walker will be asked to put up with temporary closures of overworked and eroded paths and tracks. Planning control of houses will in some cases interfere with personal taste and the freedom to build as and where one likes. These are some of the restrictions upon individual licence that are the price a co-operative public must be willing to pay to preserve the district they love.

Many associations are actively promoting this co-operation and are helping their members to acquire a deeper understanding of the countryside and its proper use. It is surely significant that the origins of some of the earliest of these are closely connected with the Lake District: the Commons, Open Spaces and Footpaths Preservation Society, the National Trust, the Lake District Safeguarding Society and later Friends of the Lake District, the Council for the Protection of Rural England — these are but a few of the associations operating locally and now strengthened by the National Parks Commission. Public awareness of threats to the environment and public support for these associations are encouraging 'signs of the times' and are much to be welcomed.

The long story of Lakeland has here been reduced to a very scant outline, just sufficient to reveal something of the amazing processes that, working through unimaginable ages have created the physical beauties of the lakes and peaks, the scenery that we love and cherish. During the last several thousand years, a mere flash in this story, this landscape has been the environment in which a wide variety of immigrants, prehistoric, Celtic, Anglian, Norse and others have found their home, have settled and have intermingled, From the mingling of these various strains has come a native Cumbrian stock in which characteristics derived from each strain can be detected, but unite to form a character that is special and distinct from that of other local populations in Britain. To this local folk the settlements among the mountains and by the lakes have become the loved homeland of many generations. We are their inheritors, and it is for us to cultivate an appreciative understanding of this heritage. We have a life tenure of it and must use it in such a way that the next generation may accept if from us in turn, not in any way depreciated but if possible enhanced by our care.

In our planning and enjoyment of the area we should think of ourselves as holding the resources and the natural beauty of Lakeland in stewardship from a long historic past and in trust for many generations to come. May that trust be informed and honourable, so that our memory is respected.

THE LIFE

The Langdale Fells and Blea Tarn

Scafell and Brown Tongue

Scale Force

Mickleden

Bow Fell

Across Ennerdale to the northern plain

Ullswater

Sheep gathered for shelter

Gable and Piers Gill

Lingmell and Scafell from Wastwater

Waterfall — Wasdale

Across Wasdale to Sellafield and the Irish Sea

Detail of St. Bees Head cliffs — current bedding

Calder Abbey — early morning

Walney

Aira Force

Storm clearing over Ullswater

Helvellyn

Striding Edge

Spindrift near Hartsop

Stockgill Force

Kentmere Reservoir

Grasmere

Iris — Loughrigg Tarn

Frozen grasses

The Langdale Pikes

Pavey Ark, Langdale

Winter sunset over Coniston

Beech trees near Coniston

Summer haze over Crummock Water

St. John's in the Vale and Blencathra

Gray Crag

Lodore Falls

Honister Pass

Buttermere and Crummock Water

River Duddon

Riggindale and Hawes Water

Harter Fell — evening

Coniston and the Old Man

Castlerigg Stone Circle near Keswick

THE LIFE

Brotherilkeld Farm, Eskdale

Newlands Valley and Scope End

Low Snab Farm — Newlands

Mrs Birkett, Round Hill Farm near Ambleside

Judith — Seatoller

Barbara, Richard, Roger and David Charnley — drinking time near Kentmere

Louise's birthday party, Kentmere Hall

Following the feed

Christine and Philip Charnley, High Oxen Fell Farm

Tom Holliday with his Limousin cattle near Coniston

Jo Woof taking lambs out of the wild

Rough Fell Sheep seeking shelter

Early steps

Eric Harrison topping up with the bottle — Eskdale

Wasdale Head Chapel

Blencow Hall

Quarry Tracks, Honister

Entrance to Road-end Level

Brian Stephenson, Keith Plaskett and David Stanger by Old Honister Mine

Clogg loading

Clogg running out of Old Honister

Jacko docking slate

Bait time

Abandoned slate quarry near Hodge Close

Abandoned copper mine near Coniston

Force Crag zinc and barytes mine in Coledale, one of the last remaining working mines

Miners drilling shot holes in Force Crag

Harold Hodgson with a cross-cut saw used for slate finishing, Skelwith Bridge

Clogg Saw

Lol Knipe — mason

Erni Rigg dressing roofing slates — Kirkstone Quarry

Blowing up slate slurry ready for disposal

Waterwheel, Little Salkeld Flour Mill

Shap granite Blue Quarry

Modern Lime Kilns, Shap

Sellafield

Preparing to lime wash Hartsop Hall

Peat mosses under Whitbarrow Scar

Forest near Thirlmere

Forester felling larch

Burning the brash

Logging by Buttermere with the water high

Clearing coppice near Sizergh

Peter Hall's Woodcraft Shop

Recaning chairs for Levens Hall

Franklin-Eldridge, wooden boatbuilders

Briggflats Meeting House, Sedbergh

Hugh Symonds, one of our top fell runners, training in the Howgill Fells

Ice Climbing on Cautley Spout, The Howgills

Climbing in Borrowdale — Falcon Crag

Quayfoot Buttress

The Raft Race — Windermere Festival

Windsurfing under the screes, Wastwater

A fish sale in Ravenglass despite the proximity of Sellafield

Char fishing, Windermere

John Elleray nets a char

The narrow gauge Ravenglass and Eskdale Railway

Gathering Sheep — Martindale

Gathering up strays

Clipping time near Kirkstone

Stan and Margaret Richardson clipping late-comers in Boredale

Loading the last bale — Windermere

Taking the wool down from Martindale ready for collection

Loading the wool on the waggon

Junior fell runner comes down off Kirk Fell

Hound trailing, Wasdale Show

Chris Hartley judging at the Wasdale Show

Ben — Patterdale sheep dog trials

Herdwicks — Kendal Auction Mart

A last Word

INDEX